WORMWOOD:

Understanding How it is Currently Impacting Earth

WORMWOOD:

UNDERSTANDING HOW IT IS CURRENTLY IMPACTING EARTH

by
Kenneth Lee Spears

Contact information:
Email -- ken.lee.spears@gmail.com

Follow on YouTube channel: "Eternal Flame of Christ"

Copyright © 2022 Kenneth Lee Spears
All rights reserved. No part of this book may be reproduced, scanned, or distributed in any printed or electronic form without permission. First Edition: MARCH 2022 Printed in the United States of America ISBN: 978-1-946826-57-2

Table of Contents

Introduction …………………………………...	1
Chapter 1: Wormwood …………………………..	3
Chapter 2: Bermuda Triangle …………………..	8
Chapter 3: Corona Virus ………………………..	10
Chapter 4: The Waters …………………………	17
Chapter 5: Noah's Flood ………………………	20
Chapter 6: Poisoned Turbulent Waters …………...	27
Chapter 7: The Dragon, Demons, and Nephilim …	36
(Chart) …………………………………..	36
Chapter 8: The Veil/Halo/Bow ………………….	46
About the Author …………………………….	57

Introduction

This book is the more in-depth follow-up book to my previous book, entitled *The Mark of the Beast is Already in Your Hand: Your Eyes See It Without Seeing It*. It will illuminate and elaborate teachings in the Bible in new ways that were always there but were unseen until now, giving reverence to the idea in the Bible of having eyes that see without seeing. I reveal hidden prophetic insight never revealed or realized before now.

If you follow these teachings, it will open a door of understanding like you've never had before and expose the truth of the Word. It will help you comprehend how the times we are living in are the prophetic times spoken of in the book of Revelation. You will begin to see and understand the scripture in deeper ways than you ever imagined.

Consider, the veil is being lifted, and a new understanding of why Jesus spoke in parables is finally being revealed. These things I show to you were shown to me by the Lord. What this will do for you is open an entirely new school of thought as it relates to scriptures, as it was meant to do. The best way to gain the most understanding while reading this is to have your Bible opened to follow along as you travel this new and exciting journey. You may likely have to revisit parts of this book to find the hidden meanings I've written into it, just as there are hidden meanings in the Bible.

Chapter 1
Wormwood

To begin this book, I need to make the most important correction of a translation that has perhaps ever been made. *WORMWOOD* was the wrong translation from ancient scriptures. The word in the original scripture is *LA'ANAH*. This word's actual translation is, "to be cursed with bitterness". I'm not sure why the scholars chose to mistranslate this to *wormwood*, but it was a lie that was perpetuated for hundreds of years. I asked the Lord when He revealed this to me, why was this so? He said these were the words that were sealed away with Daniel so that only his appointed prophet could reveal it in its time. He then told me, *"I place this mantle upon you and you will witness before Me and the truth of My Word!"*

What I experienced next was something unimaginable. I watched the 7 heavens unfold and suddenly time did not exist at all. Every event He wanted me to witness/see that has ever happened and would happen was presented before me in an instant. There are literally no words that could begin to explain the phenomena! With this explained and corrected, we would clearly be looking for a comet/star associated with a bitter curse. God revealed these things to me and much more and told me to share it with the world so they would know the times we are in. When I revealed this, Bible scholars revisited this and declared I was correct in my translation. Just before the corona virus occurred, I was shown that this star was the comet, Atlas. Atlas is believed to be a mythological Greek deity. This is important because Atlas was one of the supposed titans of Greek mythology, but what I argue is that he was one of the fallen angels and/or Nephilim mentioned in the Bible in Genesis. Further biblical proof of this can be found in the book of Job 9:9.

There is importance with the number 9 because this star falling from the heavens is found in Revelation 9, but what is most important is this is where God is explaining to Job about the Pleiades and their relationship with Atlas who is their father. With that understanding, if the Pleiades is mentioned by God, then their father Atlas must also be real, but just left out of what was allowed and accepted into scripture by the Roman Catholic church. Basically, he was left out, but his 7 daughters, the Pleiades, were allowed in. These things and much more were left out of the Holy Bible. This is only a very small fraction of the entirety of books withheld or deleted because the powers that be didn't want people to know the *'times'* in which we are living. God told me that he would give to me all the hidden knowledge to reveal these things in accordance with His Word and its truth.

Amongst all Biblical scholars, angels including Lucifer, were described as stars that fell from heaven. One must understand that also in many other pieces of scripture fallen angels are associated to stars and comets. One example of this is Revelation 1:20, the seven stars of the 7 churches are angels. Pleiades is a group of seven stars, also known as the seven 'WATER" sisters. In Job 38:31, God tells Job that he has bound them and if you read Revelation 9, you will see that these fallen angels and stars are released/unbounded. My Revelation is that the comet Atlas was the star, contrary to what people have been falsely led to believe, that would be Wormwood.

If you knew the history of Atlas you would know that he was *"cursed with a bitter curse"* to bear the weight of the heavens because of his rebellion. Some may argue that Atlas is nothing but Greek mythology, but if you know history and follow it along with the Bible you will see that Atlas was the father of the Pleiades. And if the Pleiades are mentioned three (3) times in scripture and considered truth then you must accept that their father Atlas is real.

What is called the Atlantic Ocean today was first named the Sea of Atlas, named after him. Also realize we have what are called the Florida Keys that are found in the Sea of Atlas and the star that falls from heaven is given a "Key". Keys are the small islands located off the coast of Florida. The key that God showed me was Theta Island.

Chapter 2
BERMUDA TRIANGLE

In understanding that a small island is called a Key and the Lord showed me Theta Island (Key) found in the Bermuda's 'Devil's Triangle'. God showed me that this is where Abaddon was cast into the pit and that this island is an ancient volcano.

The Lord also showed me that He named this island in His omnipotence because He is the Word just as John 1:1 says and would use this to prove His Word is truth. Theta means 9 in Greek and this is all explained in the scripture is Revelation 9. To further prove His amazing power, He showed me the comet Atlas came from the 9th star in the constellation Scorpio, which is in the scorpion's tail. It is also named Theta, "incredibly" and He told me to tell the people "As above, so below," and see that it came from the scorpion's tail just as mentioned in Rev. 9:5.

Another thing He wanted me to explain is that this island is located directly in one of the corners/angles of the Devil's Triangle, which is called Theta also from a mathematical perspective, known as the Angle of Descent (as if you will descend into the fires of Hell). Again, realize this area is an ancient volcano and can be seen with Google maps.

Chapter 3
Corona Virus

The comet, "ATLAS" was approaching Earth just before the corona virus was first beginning to reveal itself in Wuhan China. This comet, "ATLAS" and the comet "SWAN", which means "TRUMPETER", as in the angel that is a trumpeter in Revelation 8, was approaching Earth just before the corona virus was first beginning to reveal itself in Wuhan China. At the same time the largest locust plague was spreading across Africa and Asia, which is also spoken of in Rev. 9:3, further validates that this is the *'time'* we are in. This locust plague created the plague that was initially 'VSIV' which mutated and caused the swine flu that wiped out the pigs in Asia just before the Asia New Year celebration, celebrating the year of the 'pig'. This was a warning that was not heeded which led to it mutating into the Novel Corona Virus.

When this occurred, I said on my social media channel that this comet was the 'star that falls from heaven', that was misinterpreted as 'wormwood'. I said this was the judgement that was coming, and I revealed that this was the plague of locust from Revelation 9, a disease that came from a plague of locust. Many people scoffed at the case I was presenting until the CORONA VIRUS appeared in China. I then revealed this was the plague mentioned in Revelation 18 and announced a stern warning on social media that many scoffed at saying, "there is no way we are living in those days." My warning was basically this: that this was judgment for their sorcery found in Rev.18:23. One must realize China produces much of the world's so-called 'medicines' and that is the sorcery, because they actually use serpents to make it. There is a place there, Zisiqiao Village, known as the 'Snake Village', that solely harvests snake eggs to use in making vaccines. If you know anything about vaccines, you'll know that many are made by injecting a live virus into an egg and allowing it to mutate.

Commonly bird eggs are used but China decided to use snake eggs so when you get one of these vaccines you also get the egg's protein that it was cultured in, which means you get serpent DNA. This was one reason I pointed out, in accordance with Rev. 18, when it first hit China.

Another warning I gave, it states in Revelation 18:2 about how they eat every unclean and caged birds. Not long after it was announced that they were investigating the virus' origin which might have come from a wet market where they kept such unclean and caged animals to eat, including bats. I had some tell me a bat is not considered a bird. I referred those that argued against my warning to Leviticus 11:19, which showed them that Biblically a bat is considered a bird.

Realizing what I had prophesied was coming to pass, some people began to pay attention while others still scoffed. Another thing I said would occur was mentioned in

Revelation 18:17, "the merchants and ships would stand afar and watch the smoke and be scared." When travel bans began to happen, and ships could not go ashore because passengers on board were being severely affected by the virus, this prophetic word came to pass. Then my prophecy really began to be realized when they began to see the smoke from the dead bodies being burned from the plague, that was mentioned. The Lord told me to tell them in that same video, that he had sent the pig Eboli that devastated their pig population just before their Asian new year's celebration. Celebrating the year of the Pig was meant to shut down their shrines and temples and candle lighting ceremonies just as forewarned in Revelation 18:23. The Lord told me to tell them because they did not heed His warning, this was their second woe in accordance with Revelation 18.

I was told lastly to announce VERY BOLDLY that all nations would be rewarded with this plague because all had participated in her fornication. I basically said there was going to be a worldwide PANDEMIC before a single case was announced outside of China. I said all would be rewarded to the degree in which they had participated in China's (Babylon's) fornications. Almost immediately in the following days, all the church leaders and scoffers began to see that everything I had prophesied was unfolding just as I had said it would. At that point many of the same church leaders and others saw how accurate I was and began spinning their own version of my prophecy and claiming to be prophets themselves. The Lord told me that this angered Him because they were not adhering to the law of the prophets written by Moses in Jeremiah 23:30. God is against any prophets that steal prophecy from another. He told me He would change His word to give it an understanding that would leave them in such confusion that they would be as the ones mentioned in Romans 1:22, because they sought their own glory and stole prophecy from me, "His true prophet." He would show that they had no true discernment and only wanted to be recognized as a prophet when they were the ones that initially scoffed at me and now were seeking the Lord's favor after they doubted the truth of His word. God told me He would embarrass them in ways they couldn't even imagine yet.

One other major point I wanted to make about what I was shown, is the misinformation and another mistranslation that had been occurring since 2003. This has to do with what other false prophets had called Planet Nibiru, Planet X, Planet 9. See the significance and relationship to 9 again but <u>also the X is another symbol representing Theta in ancient Phoenician language.</u> It all connects back to what I was shown. What the Lord showed me was that Nibiru was never a planet. He said the ancient scrolls can prove that it was the Nibiru Point where the Euphrates and Tigris Rivers met and that this was the place where the 4 fallen angels were bound beneath the Euphrates spoken of in Revelation 9:14-15. The Lord showed me He made this with the symbol X so He could make it associate to X marks the spot like it is shown on maps. It all relates to 9 as He made it, giving reverence to His omnipotence. Understanding this will become important later in the book when I reveal the names of these fallen angels and prove that they have, in fact, been released upon the earth.

Chapter 4
THE WATERS

The same ones that initially doubted me, many who were big named ministers and others that were following me, suddenly exploded, claiming they were prophets and had the discernment of the Lord. They began telling everyone that the literal waters were about to be poisoned by the comet and that there was going to be tsunamis that would flood major parts of the planet when the comet impacted the planet. God said to just be quiet and let the false prophets put their feet in their mouths because they had stoked God's anger for falsely claiming they were prophets who had been given this prophecy which was given to me.

This is one of, if not the most important of the lessons I will teach when I reveal what was shown to me by God. What I show you through the word of God will open a door of wisdom and understanding that has never been seen or taught but has always been there right before your eyes.

Things that you saw without 'seeing' them. God led me to Revelation 17:15. What was revealed to John was that the waters spoken of in the Bible are actually the peoples, nations, multitudes, and tongues which translates into the language that is being used, remember John 1:1. God is the Word and the Word is with Him, which means He controls the language that is being used in these 'times' in which we are living. An important piece of scripture relating to this is 1 Corinthians 12:8, "For to one is given the spirit of the word of wisdom; to another the word of knowledge by the same spirit." Another supporting scripture is 1 Corinthians 12:12, "For that body is one, and hath many members, and all of the members of that one body, being many, are one body, so also is Christ." This explains that God can control the whole of the earth and events that occur through the language because we are all His body. It also says that it is important to be one with the body of Christ and His words and what they teach. To help understand this better you can go to John 4:34, where Jesus explains that he came to "finish the work of his Father". His Father's work was the Old Testament and Jesus' work was the New Testament which was his flesh and blood and his living waters as taught in John 6:56, and John 4:10. Once you read and "digest" that, you must then read John 3:5, how you must be baptized in the living waters which are the Word, both the Old and the New Testament. You will get the understanding that you must immerse yourself in the Holy Bible. Drink it up and its Spirit of Truth.

Chapter 5
NOAH'S FLOOD

Now that I've given you a very brief understanding of what the Lord showed me. I can now teach you about the truth of the flood during the time of Noah and what the Holy Bible reveals. If you go to Matthew 24:37-39 it says like in the times of Noah will be again in the time of the coming of the Son of Man. Jesus flooded the land with his words when he first came, and he will do it again in his second coming. In Verse 38 you find, "For as the days that were before the flood they were eating, drinking, and marrying…" People have fallen away from the Word. Many people are self-consumed and not eating His flesh and drinking His living waters as scripture says to do. But more importantly people will be looking for a literal flood of actual waters because they did not take the time to read and to know how to discern the Word, to see what the waters really were. I am revealing its truth now. Verse 39 says, "And (they) knew not until the flood came and took them all away." People would miss seeing the prophetic flood coming because they are looking for a flood of water, literally.

What I revealed was what was shown to John in Rev. 17:15. The waters are not actual waters. It is the peoples, nations, multitudes, and tongues/languages that are being used. Like those people who twisted my prophecy and had prophesied actual tsunamis, and such were coming, everyone is looking for actual events. They won't be paying attention to and will not see the truth of the Word that the waters are the peoples, nations, and tongues that they should be watching for. Allow me to elaborate on how and why the people will not see the "flood" coming just as Matthew 24:39 states. People would be looking for literal tsunamis and poisoned waters without realizing what the waters actually are revealed in Revelation 17:15. People are not seeing the blue and the red waves of political division that are crashing against one another in these days. They also do not see the division in the legislative and judicial "branches". As John 15:2 states, God will remove and cut away every, "branch" that does not bear His fruit. These branches are known as bodies and if you go to Matthew 12:22-28, you can see that even Jesus taught about how these bodies/houses are divided and cannot stand. Realize these bodies that are not working in the spirit/body of Christ will also fall and we are seeing this on a worldwide scale. With that explained, I would like to show you just a few examples of what you should have been looking for. Remember the statement Trump made about a storm was coming and later how people stormed the capitol, how there were new waves of infection from the Corona virus, the surge of infection, the surge in violence, the flood of immigration, and the blue wave and the red wave of the clashing political parties. It's in the peoples, nations, multitudes, and tongues/language you see the association of everything as it relates to the water. My personal favorite in proving this and my new revelation on this matter was the "Noah Vaccine Trials"! To better understand I redirect you to 1 Corinthians 12:8. Understand the spirit of the Word and its power to affect the language. You may also need to read Romans 8:1, which tells that you must walk in the spirit of the Word, His Word, the Holy Bible and not in the spirit of the flesh.

Now that I have showed you what the waters are and guided you through the shallow waters, I will take you into the deeper waters of discernment. The deeper meaning of the Word revealed to me by God. When God opened the windows of heaven and poured out the waters of heaven you then match that up with 1 Corinthians 12:8 and you'll see it was His spirit and words, which are also called His everlasting living waters. Genesis 6:17, Romans 8:1, and 1 Corinthians 12:12, all fit like puzzle pieces revealing the Truth of His Word. He destroyed all "flesh" that didn't walk in the spirit of His Word in Romans 8:1. He didn't destroy everybody just the bodies that were not of His Body, 1

Corinthians 12:12. He poured out His Spirit onto the waters/peoples, nations, multitudes, and tongues, Rev.17:15, and put it in their hearts to destroy one another, Rev.17:17, and eat its "flesh," Rev. 17:16, of all of those who do not walk in His spirit/water/words. He did this because they did not eat of His flesh as found in John 6:56.

Each of these comets were drawn into the gravitational "WAVES" of the sun and did not have the IMPACT the false prophets were proclaiming, thus making them look like fools and proving they were false prophets. Little did they realize the true discernment had been given to me. I revealed that the impact had a separate, second meaning which was to have a strong effect on someone or something, and that is when the Corona virus began. The Corona Virus was the IMPACT on and the poisoning of the waters/people.

In Revelation 17:15 it was revealed to John that the waters spoken of in the Bible were the peoples, nations, multitudes, and tongues and not literal water. Understand it is no accident that many words today are used in contexts that have a representational meaning to waters in a metaphoric sense. So rather than looking for literal waters one must be looking for metaphorical waters within the language used by people in accordance with Revelation 17:15. Just as an example, consider the gravitational "waves" of the sun that drew in the comets and the micro-"waves" it produces.

I hope you now understand why Noah's sons found wives, why the Earth is so populated with diversity, and why Genesis says there were Nephilim before the flood and after. It wasn't a literal flood it was God opening the heavens and pouring out His spirit which is the Word. With that understood, the ones that were destroyed were the ones walking in the flesh and not in the spirit, because it clearly states all "flesh" was destroyed, not everybody. This can also be confirmed in Acts 2:17, where it says in the last days, He will pour out His spirit. It is important to understand Ecclesiastes 1:9, "what has been done will be done again." The Lord's truth reveals itself and all hidden knowledge if you can discern the Word. Scripture states God is the harvester of harvesters. Any farmer will tell you that when there has been a severe drought it makes the water table drop too low. Then they must flood the field in order to return the land back to a state where they can plant their seeds in hopes of having a crop to harvest. Therefore, God must pour out His waters/words/spirit and flood the land with it and then the gospel will begin to be taught throughout the world to all nations, peoples, multitudes, and tongues.

CHAPTER 6
POISONED TURBULENT WATERS

Picking up from the last chapter, 'God pouring out His spirit' found in Acts 2:17, can also be confirmed and linked to Romans 2:8, where He will pour out His wrath on the wicked and Romans 14:10, how man will drink the wine of His wrath because they did not drink of His waters like it was taught to the Samaritan woman in John 4. More importantly the current state the world is in, as it relates to scripture is Rev. 16:4-6, when the vial poured out by the third angle on the rivers, fountains, and waters which are actually people, nations, multitudes, and tongues revealed to John in Rev. 17:15. As I have previously shown, it was Atlas and the Pleiades that were cursed with bitterness and being that they are both associated with the sea and waters they passed their bitterness onto the people. This began with the poison of the Coronavirus but also the bitterness and division of the waters/peoples like the blue waves and red waves of the

Democratic and Republican parties, but on a worldwide level. Cities began to be burned and destroyed which was prophesied in Revelation 17:16, the very next verse, giving even further proof that these times we live in parallel to scripture. The division now happening is important because I revealed something very new and never understood regarding the Leviathan mentioned in the Bible, Job chapter 41. I revealed that the sea monster was a serpent-like beast in its behavior and words that are in the sea/waters/peoples, nations, multitudes, and tongues stir up the waters/people with their tongues, Job 41:31. The "LEVI"-athan is the tribe of LEVI of our times. Just like there are the Thessalonians, Corinthians, there are Leviathans.

The Leviathans, in the time of Moses were the Levites lead by Aaron, the ones that sowed discord among the people while Moses was on the mountain. They convinced the people to turn to wicked, ungodly ways and commit idolatry. The way to see what I revealed and taught, is to understand it in a new way -- that they are a mirage. They give false words/waters that lead people into the desert/dry places and do not quench thirst as opposed to the everlasting living word/waters of the Holy Bible that was taught to the Samaritan woman in John 4. This can be understood from the perspective of Aaron, when he was with Moses and the Israelites and they were led into the desert/dry places under the guidance of Aaron and the tribe of Levi, the first Leviathans. Realize that the church was always taught to be the rock and the foundation, and the Levites were the first rock/*church*. Moses had to strike the rock/*Levites* with his staff to bring forth waters for the people so that their thirst might be quenched and to bring them out of those dry places they had been led into by the mirage of the Leviathans (this can be found taught in Numbers chapter 20:10-11). The support of my new teaching and revelation regarding this, can be found in Exodus chapter 15. The Israelites were in the wilderness and had no water but, "bitter" waters to drink and

Moses had to throw in a bush to make the waters sweet. Another factor you can use to verify this is to look at the description of the Leviathan in Job 41. It talks about making a covenant with him and how he will make many supplicate unto him with his soft words. It's clear this is speaking of a man that is like Satan in nature. Also note how his armor is very similar to the armor of God taught of in Ephesians 6:11-18. One last example is found in Leviticus 10, when the sons of Aaron were destroyed by the Lord for sacrilegious behaviors against God. It speaks of a WAVE offering in that chapter also and its relationship to waters. Can you now see the symbolism in the Bible that supports these new revelations of hidden truth and its significance that only I was able to reveal in the Word?

This was and is still occurring on a global level. This was the bitterness that is alluded to in scripture that wormwood would cause in the waters/people and would poison the people and cause them to burn the cities and make people turn against one another. Understand it's seen in the tongues/language just as in Revelation 17:15. The statement Donald Trump made about how a storm was coming or how he said he was going to, "drain the swamp waters", and his campaign slogan, "come hell or high water". You must see it in the language not as literal waters, and this is why it was shown to John in this manner, that in its given time only the Lord's true appointed prophet would be able to discern the truth while false prophets would be speaking of literal waters. Don't forget about Joe Biden's campaign slogan which was "battle for the soul of the nation". This ultimately led to the "storming of the capitol". The blue and red waves swept over America. We also saw the "flood of immigration". This can be compared to the concept from another new understanding I have taught, how waters/people, nations, and tongues can become poisoned/polluted/stirred up by a flood of people who don't share American values and/or either bring into the nation a "surge" of violence and the increasing crime "wave" across the country. It was never meant to mean literal waters, and therefore the peoples would not see it coming since they couldn't discern. False prophets would be teaching actual waters but thanks to what was revealed to me well over a year ago, I was able to warn the people of the misinterpretation and show the truth of the Word and the true discernment. The Lord made me hold back on revealing the truth just long enough to let the false prophets prophesy about actual flooding, so they could be uncovered as the false prophets spoken of in Matthew 24:24.

During that time, I felt a heavy yoke upon me. I had many church leaders questioning my discernment and I began to question myself, so I asked the Lord to please give me another sign of these times. He said, *fear not*, that He, *"through me"* would
show more of the *truth of His Word* and that through me, He would manifest the truth of 1 Corinthians 1:20. The church

leaders who believed themselves wise would be made fools. I was also shown that God would use this pandemic to shut the doors of the churches that had led people away from His Word. It would give people a chance to get away from false doctrines and get back to reading His Word, the Holy Bible, for themselves and regain a personal relationship with *Him/the Word* John1:1.

At this point He sent the sign I had asked for. The comet Swan appeared. God told me to now explain and show that the other name for a swan is a *"trumpeter"* and that it was one of the 7 stars/angels from Revelation chapter 1 and 8. I heard God say this is the third time He has had to release this revelation because no one saw or heard the first 2 times which were the warnings. He said, "their eyes see without seeing and hear without hearing" and that mankind had accepted evil and the false doctrines of man. God is going to release the evil so mankind will open their eyes and ears to

His truth and see the mercy and grace He has lovingly given for so long that has not been reciprocated.

The significance of this comet is that it is symbolic of Apollyon/Abaddon from Revelation 9:11. More importantly it came from the constellation Swan, which is better known as the Northern Cross. Also important is this constellation is where the veil, Nebula, is located which will be relevant later in this book in the chapter discussing the veil.

It was at this time I announced the corona virus would become a pandemic and span the entire earth as part of God's Judgement. I did this on my social media before a single case was found outside of China. I have time-stamped video proof of this prophecy. When this prophecy came to pass many of these long-time church leaders realized I truly had a prophetic gift. What became sad was that many of these same ones began using my prophetic visions and claimed themselves to be prophets to capitalize on what I was revealing while claiming it as their own prophecy. They began telling people they were having dreams about tsunamis, and the waters being poisoned and undrinkable. This angered God greatly because they were not given this prophecy so He told me this was where He would show that they were fools and not His prophets as in Romans 1:22. God said these men were only **"PROFITS"** and not His **"PROPHETS"** and to show these two words, and how He created them so that they could be distinguished.

CHAPTER 7
The Dragon, Demons, and Nephilim

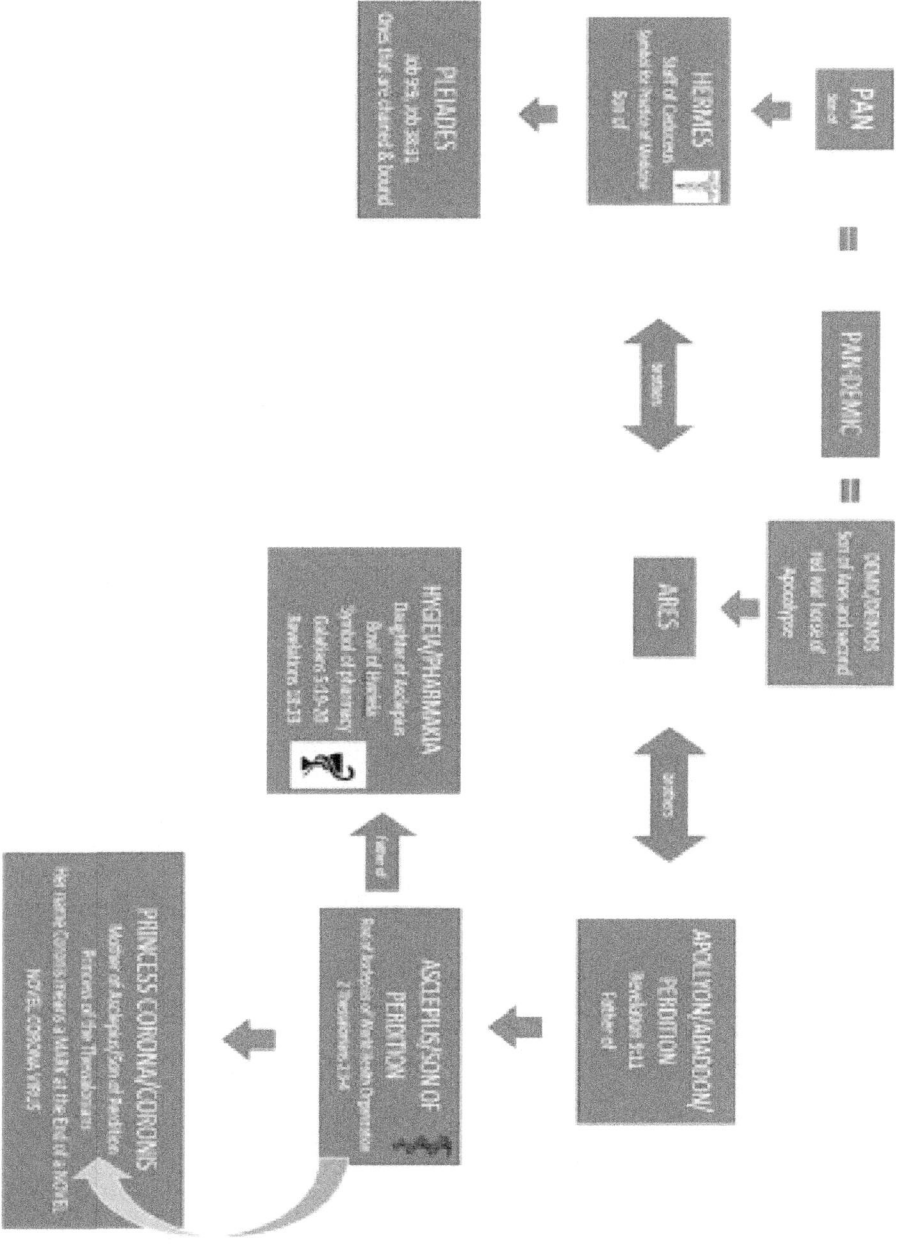

I wanted to first show this chart from my previous book to use as a guide to show the interconnected relationships of these fallen ones and Nephilim that are at work in these times.

It is important because the Bible doesn't reveal many of these demons and who or what they are. This was done so that Satan could not conceal things but so that only God's appointed could reveal things in accordance with His Word giving reverence to its truth. I want to begin with the dragon himself. If I said we are in the end times as I have, then surely **the Dragon** that is spoken of in Revelation 13 would have to be here. It was "Dragon 13 naturally speaking and Dragon 13 full power integrated software"! This dragon gives power to the RAM (Random Access Memory) in your phones to speak back to you, (see it in the language), the Dragon gives the image/IM·AGE (Instant Memory Age), "the power to speak" just as stated in Revelation 13. Also, in that chapter it says the beast is like a lamb and a RAM is like a ram. As a matter of fact, a young male lamb is even called a lamb ram. The language used in scripture was to reveal these things that will be.

I showed in my previous book the image that is worshiped was your **cell phone**, which is also where you find the mark in your right hand, the Bluetooth symbol located in your phone, which is always in your hand day and night. Notice how people worship their phones. The worst thing you can do to most people is take away their phones. Many will not give them up and wouldn't know how to function without them. More importantly it has the power to speak just as prophesied in Revelation 13. The dragon and that beast are here. The other beast that comes out of the waters/peoples, "multitudes, nations, and tongues was also the 7 heads of this beast that represents the 7 continent/peoples, nations, multitudes, and tongues. This represents the Leviathans that are stirring up the people/waters with their tongues/language. Race and hate baiting posturing everyone against one another (Luke 12:53) and nation against nation (Matthew 24:7).

The next thing I'd like to point out is what I revealed in my previous book, the arrival of the second horseman of the Apocalypse which was **Ares**. I already showed that I knew it was his arrival when they announced the Pandemic, but I also knew because they implemented draconian measures. To understand this, you must discern words and how these evolved which was what Isaiah 46:9-10 alluded to. Remember their ancient meanings and what was said in Revelation 6. Each time a horse is shown to John, the beast which is associated to the serpent tells him "To see"! With that understood, I can now reveal that the word draconian measures announced came from the more ancient word Drakon, which was serpent, and the word Drakon came from the word Drakien, which means, "to see". With that one announcement, they announced "to see the serpent" which is how scriptures announce the horsemen's arrival.

The demon I wanted to show in association to Ares was his sister, **Eris**. She goes wherever he goes and was responsible for contention and strife. Obviously, there is no question we are seeing this since the pandemic began, thus proving what I was shown. Strife and contention are defined as bitterness and is exactly what was stated would happen to the waters/people because of wormwood's affects. The strife we are seeing in the streets because of the pandemic's arrival, are Ares and his sister, Eris. Psalm 55:9, is the Biblical proof of this. It very clearly stated the destruction of the cities with violence and strife and its relationship to the tongues/language that was being used can be further affirmed and tested against what was shown to John in Revelation 17:15, and Luke 12:49. Unequivocal sound doctrinal proof.

The next demon I want to reveal that has been unbounded and released is "**Erra**". This demon was responsible for pestilence and political confusion. There should be no question that he is at work considering the coronavirus and the confusion with the latest election cycle between Donald Trump and Joe Biden. This demon was poured out with the third vial from Revelation 16:4. Remember the waters are the people, nation, and multitude tongues (Revelation 17:15). He was in a sense the corona virus itself. The Lord showed me there was a significance to his name. Erra is sounded the same but with an added R in comparison to the word Era. This was done to prove He is the word just as John 1:1 stated. He did this so I could show people the era in which we live while giving reference of how He can reveal things through words, including the names of demons that would attempt to conceal themselves.

The demon that I reveal next was a cousin to the Pleiades from Job 38:31. This demon, like Pleiades, has the ability to affect the waters/people, but also actual waters. This is one of the ones released from the Nibiru Point of the 2 rivers I mentioned earlier where the Tigris and the

Euphrates meet which was spoken of in Revelation 9:14-15. She was connected to being bound beneath the rivers. She has the ability to create famine by flooding the rivers, and this has been seen worldwide. Rivers worldwide have flooded crops and livestock creating long term food shortages in many places. Her name was "**Eurynome**" which is pronounced the same as "your enemy". There again is the word play just like the demon Erra. Just as the pandemic began, the entire area known as the wheat belt in America flooded. This flood destroyed millions of crops, silos of reserve foods, and livestock. At the same time there was major flooding from Three Gorges Dam, Yangtze, and other major rivers and tributaries across China. This has created major problems for China and its food supplies and economy. All of this was this demon's doing.

The demon shown to me next was **Hephaestus**. This demon is associated with Eurynome through her daughter, Aglaea, who is the consort of Hephaestus who provokes him into acting. He is the demon of fire, volcanoes, and earthquakes and there is no doubt we have seen this increase since the comet Atlas and Swan appeared. America, Greece, Australia, and Russia especially have experienced historical fires just in the last year and a half. The undeniable proof was said in mythology that you would know he had been released when Mt. Etna erupted and that occurred December 2020. He was said to have been bound under Mt. Etna and when it erupted, he was released. These are, just to name a few, of the main demons that have been released. I've given these specifically to prove the truth of the word from Matthew 24:7, and Luke 21:11. In reiterating my argument from my previous book. You may say these are Greek deities, but I declare they are the fallen angels and their Nephilim offspring that are specifically spoken of in scripture. The Bible specifically names Apollyon in Revelation 9:11, and Pleiades in Job 9:9, and Job 38:31. If they are mentioned then their brothers, sisters, and children must be real as well. They were simply not specifically named as these two were.

One last notable demon I want to mention is **Scotus**. This deity is clearly present in these times. "SCOTUS" is the acronym for the Supreme Court Justice of The United States. This specific demon was known for bringing dark times and this can easily be seen in the laws of the land that no longer represent Christian values. Laws like allowing abortion. SCOTUS was present and recognized as a dark spirit in the time that the Ancient Roman empire fell. This was not revealed until now, through me. The most interesting aspect of this demon is that it dates further back. It was known as Erebus and the 9 gods of Ennead during the Ancient Egyptian period when it fell. Realize the 9 of Ennead as it relates to the 9 Supreme Court Justices. This was the entity that was the plague of darkness that was spoken of in Exodus 10. This was known as the ninth plague of Egypt as it relates to 9 as well. This demon created a deep darkness over a land before its fall. An overshadowing of dark times.

Notice again we are brought back to 9/ Theta/ X. See that The Lord did in fact give a means to identify these fallen ones and reveal all of this in a way that only His true prophet could interpret. Only His true prophet could be recognized above all the false prophets living in these days which was also said would occur in Matthew 24:24. The many false prophets of these times that are and have been prophesying for and promoting their false savior, A-BAD-"DON" in Revelation 9:11, when Psalm 146:3 tells us to not put your faith in a leader because they cannot save.

CHAPTER 8
The Veil/Halo/Bow

The only way you will fully grasp what I am about to reveal is that you must first try and comprehend the omnipotence of God. He is all powerful, in all places, in all things, at all times. In simplest terms He is multi-faceted in ways unimaginable to the human mind. I'm going to give what I consider a simple single word and understanding that scholars have tried to figure out this truth for thousands of years. It was fully revealed to me by the Lord, who gave it to me to share with the world.

To first be able to wrap your mind around this, I want to explain these somewhat basic concepts. The veil and bow are, "the simplest of fabrics" as spoken of and taught through scripture. I was shown this was the "fabric of society" which can be found in 2 Corinthian 3:7-18. The Lord showed this to me and said that in these days the world was seeing this very thing occur globally because of their falling away and moral decay. The veil/ society being torn apart as when the veil was torn in the temple as Jesus gave up the spirit on the cross. Halo, an Arc, a rain "bow", the "bow" of a ship, and the Seal of the Covenant shown to Noah after the flood of the waters. Hence the name rain/water, bow/an arc in its relationship to water. All these are one in the same and multi-faceted. Another thing to understand was what the Bible said, "Like in the days of Noah, it will be again at the coming of Jesus Christ." With that you should be able to discern there will be a flood and as I've already taught the waters aren't literal waters. They are the peoples, nations, multitude and tongues, the language. I've already shown what we are seeing in the people's language about the waters, waves, floods, and surge. One other important piece of scripture I want you to understand is Revelation 7:3, when the angels were told to "seal" up the foreheads of true Christians. Remember seal is also bow, halo, and arc.

What you see depicted in many ancient pictures are halos around the heads of Godly anointed people. Scholars always gave no recognition to halos because they said they are mentioned nowhere in the Bible, but I'm going to prove it, unequivocally. The word halo comes from a combining of two words. One is halophyte which means "salt" and the word halogen which means "light". This is found in Mathew 5:13, you are the "salt" and the "light" of the earth. That's just one proof. Secondly, the word halo in Greek means "threshing floor". That can be found many times in the Bible and both meanings, I've just proven, are very significant to these times. First, the salt that is in our bodies is strontium. Strontium salt crystals that have a piezo-electromagnetic effect. What's even more revealing about this is that strontium is found in its most concentrated form in a mineral called celestite which comes from the word celestial. This salt was what makes us the celestial beings and bodies. The misunderstanding was that the angels are the celestial beings, but I've shown you that we are. This is what made Lucifer jealous of us and why he wanted to destroy us.

One of the ways Satan is currently trying to destroy us is by injecting aluminum salt into us through the injections the powers that be are trying to force us to take relating to the corona virus. Vaccines contain aluminum salts which are not our natural salts and may cause you to do something called 'calcium dump'. This makes you lose your natural salt which is specifically warned of in Mathew 5:13-16, about your salt losing its natural saltiness, which causes you to lose your light/halo, celestial essence.

Another facet was the fact it is a 'threshing floor'. What was shown to me was how it acts to separate the chaff from the grain, the flesh from the spirit. As I've stated we have our celestial bodies and the halo that we are given will be given to us by the other celestial bodies that already have halos, the sun and the moon and their "waves". Notice the language/tongues that again associate to waters but aren't actual waters. They are gravitational and microwaves and the gravitational is magnetic which interacts with out strontium which is also magnetic. Realize the sun and moon both have halos that are created from water crystals and the gravitational waves affects the waters on earth but also us, just as Revelation 17:15 stated, we are the waters that were shown to John. This can be understood because the moon cycles control the tides of the seas and oceans.

I'm going to reveal now many secrets and revelations like no other has had, shown to me by the Lord. As I said in the beginning of this chapter these halos of these celestial bodies are also a rain-"bow" which was also an arc like as in an Ark. Therefore, the rainbow mentioned in Genesis that was shown to Noah and reiterated in Revelation 4:1-4, was extremely significant because it showed that John was transformed into spirit speaking with an angel/trumpet of the Lord that called him up to the heavens. We know through scripture we will be called up to the heavens and we also know that the Lord's angels will seal up the foreheads of God's children as in Revelation 7:3. I reveal now to you, this, the hidden truth that was always there to be seen but only revealed to me. This was what most now call and see as the rapture event that will occur. It is the next arc that we will enter in the second flood. It is a halo, the salt and the light, an arc and as it relates to a bow, like the bow of a ship, but also it is the bow that the rider on the first horse of the apocalypse has. This was never understood until now and watch how it all comes together as I reveal more.

The rain-"bow" shown to Noah was called the "seal" of the covenant and a promise to never actually flood the earth again. It's also the seal that will seal up the foreheads of God's children in the end. A rain-bow/halo/arc/seal of the foreheads spoken of in Revelation chapter 7. Other evidence that was shown to me to prove this was Revelation 22:13. The Lord stated, "He was the first and last." The first horseman sealing and protecting the children of God and the last 5th horseman that destroyed all the wicked with his sword. The first horseman doesn't have arrows with his bow because it was never a bow as in a weapon that needed arrows. It was the bow that I have now revealed.

As one place of reference you can go to Revelations 10:1 and see that there is an angel spoken of with a rainbow above its head. The more important scripture I refer you to is Revelations 6:2. In the original Greek translation the word used to express white is 'toxon' and that translates into a brilliant light. In its most ancient form, it translates into a rainbow or arc. See that yet again I have revealed ancient secrets that were unknown until now through my revelation.

How all this relates to the sun and moon, halos, and veil, in scripture can be found in the gospel of Luke describing the crucifixion of Jesus. It describes how the sun was darkened for three hours and in the earliest translation was written as *"heliou eklipontos"* which translates to eclipse of the sun. When this occurs, you have the gravitational waves of the sun and moon directed on one area, known to have devastating effects to the tectonic plates creating major earthquakes and this happened upon his death, and it is recorded.

The significance was the two celestial bodies, sun and moon came together creating a darkness while at the same time emitted a certain light from both of their halos coming together all at once, it was at this very moment that everyone saw prophecy fulfilled from Psalms 148:3-4. The sun, moon, and stars and their waters BOWED to him. This was the moment that placed a veil upon the world. This was why the veil of the temple was torn in two. It signified the release of the Holy Spirit into the earth, the splitting of the first church into the second church which is Christianity, and a veil of protection and salvation to all that declare Jesus Christ as Lord and Savior. He used the waters, "gravitational and micro- waves" to connect His Holy Spirit to us in that moment He gave up His spirit to us, Matthew 27:50-51. To understand this in the most basic sense you can go to 1 John 1:5-7. This teaches about walking in the light and how it will cleanse us. When you walk in the light of the sun or moon its light shines on you. That was also the water, and its waves wash over and cleanse you if you have the Word of God in you. This is what seals up your forehead.

Another way shown to me to help people understand this is by means of the Archangels. The word itself is, "ARC" with a silent "H." but more importantly sounded and pronounced, "ARK" just like everything I've shown. These archangels are God's crowning achievement among angels, His actual crown, and are His halo in heaven. They are the seraphim that are the only ones that are allowed in direct presence of the God. These are also the ones that will be sent out to gather the elect and seal up the foreheads of the chosen with that halo/ARK found in Matthew 24:31, Mark 13:27, and Revelation 7:3. These angels will be sent to gather the elect unto them, their arc, thus sealing and protecting them and this will be what many have not fully understood until now as the 'rapture'. The meaning behind it all was lost completely. The true meaning was an amazing story of complete love, mercy, compassion, and salvation. Jesus is going to pour out his spirit on all flesh causing a complete cleansing so that we will no longer walk in flesh but only in spirit. He is going to wash away all wickedness with his spirit because we will no longer have any fleshly desires to feel, chase, lust after, or entertain. We will be flooded with his word and all its truth and glory. Acts 2:17, John 14:26, and Joel 2:28, all testify to what will happen. We won't even need a book, the Bible, because every word of it will live inside us.

With that understood see that is His light/halo/rainbow/arc that we will enter into just like in the times of Noah. Noah entered an ark, and we will enter an arc. Just like in Noah's time all flesh was destroyed, our flesh and fleshly desires will be gone which is what leads to sin. We will only be spiritual, celestial beings and will be walking with Jesus in spirit. It is ultimately such an amazing story of compassion, mercy, and salvation.

About the Author

Kenneth Lee Spears is a well-recognized Christian author and Biblical scholar. He has accurately retranslated many things in scripture that had previously been mistranslated for thousands of years. Kenneth is the only recognized prophet that prophesied the pandemic, vaccine, and all the events that have occurred from that point. His YouTube channel, *Eternal Flame of Christ*, gives absolute proof to these claims. As a born-again Christian he has given the world an entirely new understanding of scripture by revealing ancient things which were given to him by the Lord through wisdom and knowledge.

Made in the USA
Middletown, DE
10 February 2023